UNDERSTANDING THE IMPORTANCE OF CARING FOR OUR CLERGY

IN THE CUMBERLAND PRESBYTERIAN CHURCH

MANUAL

FOR PRESBYTERIAL COMMITTEES ON CLERGY CARE OR COMMITTEES ON MINISTRY

Pastoral Development Ministry Team
Cordova (Memphis), Tennessee
2020

A publication of the Pastoral Development Ministry Team of the Cumberland Presbyterian Church by the Communications Ministry Team, CPC, and distributed by Cumberland Presbyterian Resources of the Discipleship Ministry Team, CPC.

The Pastoral Development Ministry Team of the Ministry Council of the Cumberland Presbyterian Church is the successor organization to the Committee on the Ministry of the Cumberland Presbyterian Church.

Funded, in part, by your contributions to Our United Outreach.

First Edition 2020

ISBN: 978-1-945929-28-1

DEDICATION

This manual is dedicated to all the former executive directors and team leaders of the Commission on the Ministry/Pastoral Development Ministry Team.

- The Reverend Doctor James Knight, Executive Director of the Commission on the Ministry (June 1992-December 2000)
- The Reverend Doctor James M. Searcy, Executive Director of the Commission on the Ministry (February 2001-February 2003)
- The Reverend Doctor Chris Joiner, Executive Director of the Commission on the Ministry (March 2003-June 2004)
- The Reverend Stephanie Brown, Executive Director of the Commission on the Ministry/Pastoral Development Ministry Team Leader (January 2005-July 2009)
- The Reverend Doctor Milton L. Ortiz, Pastoral Development Ministry Team Leader (December 2009-April 2014)
- The Reverend Chuck Brown, Pastoral Development Ministry Team Leader (October 2014-April 2017)

I would like to acknowledge in particular the Reverend James (Jim) Searcy, who became Executive Director while I served alongside him as associate pastor at the Dyersburg Cumberland Presbyterian Church, Dyersburg, Tennessee. He was my mentor and friend and was the absolute best mentoring pastor to this novice. I was a member of the Commission on the Ministry when he was hired as the Executive Director. I remember sitting in that meeting with tears in my eyes, knowing what I was losing as an associate pastor, but knowing the wonderful gift of leadership the Cumberland Presbyterian Church was going to receive. Unfortunately, Jim served the denomination for only a brief period of time before a debilitating stroke forced him to retire. To this day, I am surrounded by his leadership, support and friendship. In fact, my office at the denominational center holds the beautiful hand-crafted bookcases that he made while he was Director. Thank you, Jim for your wisdom, love, guidance, and patience. You have touched the lives of many pastors.

The Reverend Doctor Pam Phillips-Burk

TABLE OF CONTENTS

ACKNOWLEDGMENTS

Special thanks and appreciation to the Pastoral Development Ministry
team elected members who were instrumental in the development of
this manual:
Reverend Lisa Anderson
Reverend Amber Clark
Reverend Paul Earheart-Brown
Reverend Matthew Ingram
Reverend Duawn Mearns
Reverend Sandra Shepherd
and
Rev. Shelia O'Mara, Liaison as 189th Moderator of the General Assembly.
Thank you for sharing your ideas, for endless proofreading, and for
sticking with the project until it was completed.

In addition, our team would like to acknowledge the presbyterial
committees who are responsible for the support and care of ordained
clergy. In some cases, this might be the Committee on the
Ministry/Preparation. In other presbyteries, it is a committee dedicated
to this responsibility. We hope this manual will be a useful resource to
do your job effectively. We are always open to your ideas and feedback
for future resources and ministries. Thank you for all the work you do
on behalf of the Cumberland Presbyterian ministers in your
presbyteries.

INTRODUCTION

CONGRATULATIONS! Your presbytery has determined that it is important to have a Clergy Care Committee to offer support and encouragement to the ordained ministers under their care. This manual is for members of a committee tasked with that role. In presbyteries that do not have a separate committee for this task, whatever committee is in place for preparation and oversight will find this a helpful resource. The manual is more appropriate for presbyteries within the United States, but many of the ideas and suggestions can be helpful in a wide variety of contexts. Any contract samples or items related to insurance, benefits, or salary would be subject to each country's legal system and laws.

This manual is certainly not an exhaustive resource but is designed to provide ideas and stimulate a committee's creativity in providing ongoing support, encouragement and ministry. The most important thing a committee can do is to establish a relationship with the ministers in your presbytery through good communication, support and encouragement. Continue to hold up before ministers the importance of their call, which can and does change throughout their career; therefore, it is helpful to honor and celebrate their call. A healthy relationship between the Committee on Clergy Care and the ministers can have a profoundly positive impact upon the minister, the congregation, the presbytery, and the Kingdom of God.

Many of the responsibilities of a Clergy Care Committee are taken from *The Presbytery Manual of Operations*, which was approved by the 1988 General Assembly. (The Presbytery Manual of Operations, page 12-13. Manual is on the General Assembly website - www.cumberland.org/gao/presbytery/PRESBYTERY_MANUAL_OF_OPE RATION.pdf). There are references also from General Assembly minutes and the "Constitution."

The Manual of Operations did not separate responsibilities between two different committees. This manual contains those responsibilities that are more reflective of the care and support for the ordained clergy. This manual completes a three-book series:

> Book One: *Understanding God's Call to the Ministry of Word and Sacrament in the Cumberland Presbyterian Church: Guide for Inquirers*
> Book Two: *Understanding the Process for Ordination in the Cumberland Presbyterian Church for Presbyterial Committees on the Ministry or Preparation for the Ministry*
> Book Three: *Understanding the Importance of Caring for Our Clergy in the Cumberland Presbyterian Church: Manual for Presbyterial Committees on Clergy Care or Committees on Ministry*

The Pastoral Development Ministry Team (PDMT) welcomes your feedback and input on how to improve this manual and in turn strengthen our work with the ordained clergy within the Cumberland Presbyterian denomination.

SUMMARY OF
CUMBERLAND PRESBYTERIAN STRUCTURE AND POLITY

In the Presbyterian system of government, the **presbytery** is the key unit. **Ministers of the Word and Sacrament** hold membership in the presbytery and not in a particular church. Only the presbytery has the authority to **receive candidates** for the ministry and to guide and nurture them toward ordination. This guidance is offered through the presbytery's **Committee on the Ministry/Preparation**.

Only the presbytery has the authority to organize new churches. Other responsibilities that belong uniquely to the presbytery include establishing and dissolving pastoral relationships; uniting, dividing, and dissolving churches; taking oversight of churches without pastors and appointing a moderator for their session; and electing commissioners to General Assembly. Presbytery typically meets twice a year (based upon presbytery's standing rules).

The membership of the presbytery consists of its ordained ministers and representatives for the sessions of its particular churches. (*Confession*, 2.4) Ministers shall attend all meetings of the presbytery, or present to the stated clerk a valid reason for their absence. (*Confession*, 2.51)

SPECIFIC RESPONSIBILITIES OF A
CLERGY CARE COMMITTEE

The Clergy Care Committee shall consist of six members in three staggered terms. The number may be more or less than six as determined by the presbytery and included in the Standing Rules (*Confession*, 5.41). The terms shall be for three years, and members may not serve more than three consecutive terms (*Confession*, 5.42). The committee should include both ordained ministers and laypersons, and at least one of the laypersons should be an elder. (*Confession*, 5.43) The stated clerk should be an advisory member of the committee (*Confession*, 5.44).

The committee will need to have a **chairperson/facilitator** and a **secretary/recorder**. The chairperson, in partnership with the committee will set the agenda for each meeting and see that it is sent to the members in a timely fashion. The recorder will take minutes of the meetings and distribute those to the members following the meeting. The recorder will also send a report to the Presbytery Clerk to be included in the preliminary minutes. Presbytery may have a set date that all committees meet. If not, then the Clergy Care Committee will need to decide when and how often to meet in order to conduct business.

This manual is intended to help the committee address the responsibilities detailed in the *Presbytery Manual of Operations* (found online at www.cumberland.org/gao. Below is a summary of those responsibilities, which are expanded upon later in the manual.

1. The committee is responsible for monitoring the freedom of the pulpits in the presbytery. Ministers should be responsible in their

preaching, but neither the session nor members of the congregations should be allowed to interfere with the ministers' freedom to preach the gospel.

2. The committee is responsible for monitoring the ministries of the various pastors in the presbytery. When a problem arises which cannot be resolved within the session, the committee should investigate the situation and seek reconciliation. If not possible, the committee should report the matter to the presbytery making such recommendations as it deems advisable. It is preferable for the session to seek the committee's help in such situations, but if such an invitation is not forthcoming, the committee should initiate the action. Because problems involving the pastor involve the congregation, it is important that the committee work closely with the Board of Missions. (See Manual of Operations, 5.25)

3. The committee shall encourage the ministers of the presbytery to participate in programs of continuing education and work with the General Assembly's Pastoral Development Ministry Team (PDMT) and Memphis Theological Seminary (MTS) in making such programs available.

4. Situations which may call for the disciplining of a minister should be reported to the presbytery. The procedures for handling such cases are stated in the "Rules of Discipline," especially in the sections 3.401-3410 - "Specific Procedures for Ministers."

5. The committee should publicize and promote seminars that deal with marital problems, marriage enrichment, and coping with the unique problems of the ministerial family.

6. The committee shall encourage ministers and/or spouses who are having trouble coping to seek professional help. The committee should provide information concerning the availability of such help, and where possible, provide financial support for such services.

7. The committee shall investigate reports concerning ministers who flagrantly disregard the provisions of the "Constitution" of the Cumberland Presbyterian Church and/or preach and teach doctrines contrary to the creedal statement of the church.

8. Report to the presbytery annually the type of ministry in which each minister on the presbytery roll is engaged. Presbytery has

responsibility to review and possibly approve the work of ministers who are not engaged in generally recognized forms of ministry.

9. Require annual reports from ministers whose ministry is not under the jurisdiction of the presbytery. Presbytery has responsibility to require that all ministers engage in the work of the church unless honorably retired or excused from the presbytery.

10. Receive and review annual reports from the sessions on the pastors' compensation, and present to presbytery requests for changes in terms of the pastors' calls.

11. Prepare annual necrology report for the memorial service at presbytery.

HELPFUL TERMS

Clergy Crisis Fund – Fund that provides financial support to clergy who are in crisis and in need of support and care.

Committee on the Ministry (Preparation) – Presbytery's agency for the oversight of ministerial probationers and ordained clergy, unless those responsibilities have been assigned to a Clergy Care Committee or another committee.

Confession of Faith **(1984)** – Creedal statement and government standards for the Cumberland Presbyterian Church and Cumberland Presbyterian Church in America. The five major divisions are: *Confession of Faith*, "Rules of Discipline," "Rules of Order," "Constitution," "Directory of Worship."

Constitution – Document contained in the *Confession of Faith*, delineating the government of the Cumberland Presbyterian Church and Cumberland Presbyterian Church in America.

Employee Assistance Program (EAP) – Counseling program provided at no cost to the minister who may be experiencing issues in their family or relationships, grief, psychological stress, alcohol or drug abuse. Benefits apply to the minister's family and all who live in the household. Most presbyteries are participants in the program.

General Assembly – Highest judicatory of the Cumberland Presbyterian Church representing in one body all the particular churches thereof. It bears the title of the General Assembly of the Cumberland Presbyterian Church/Cumberland Presbyterian Church in America and constitutes the bond of union, peace, correspondence and mutual confidence among all its churches and judicatories.

Memphis Theological Seminary (MTS) – A graduate school of theology affiliated with the Cumberland Presbyterian Church located in Memphis, Tennessee.

Minister of Word and Sacrament – A person who has been ordained in the ministry of the Cumberland Presbyterian Church or the Cumberland Presbyterian Church in America. A Minister of Word and Sacrament can serve in a variety of roles and settings – associate/assistant pastor, co-pastor, pulpit supply, interim pastor, chaplain, academic professor, or denominational employee. Presbytery recognizes a minister's call to a particular ministry.

- **Bi-vocational** – A pastor that serves a congregation less than full-time and works a secular job at the same time.
- **Chaplain** (military, hospital, hospice, prison, academic, other setting).
- **Honorably Retired** – A status granted upon action of the presbytery. While still a minister, she/he no longer is required to attend presbytery or serve on a committee.
- **Interim** – A pastor that serves in between installed pastors for a period of 6 months or less. The status is approved by presbytery and can be renewed, if needed. An interim pastor cannot be installed as the pastor of the congregation.
- **Stated Supply** – An ordained minister, licentiate, or a candidate approved by presbytery to serve as minister of a particular church (congregation). A stated supply is not an installed pastor and may perform only those pastoral functions set forth in the "Constitution."

Pastor – Ordained minister who has been installed by the presbytery to provide spiritual leadership in a particular congregation.

Associate/Assistant Pastor – Ordained minister who has been installed by the presbytery to assist the pastor in providing spiritual leadership in a particular church.

Pastoral Development Ministry Team (PDMT) – Ministry Council team that provides nurture and care for ordained ministers and probationers, and resources and events to improve their pastoral ministry. The team works in close partnership with the presbytery Committee on the Ministry/Preparation/Clergy Care.

Presbytery – Primary governing body within the Cumberland Presbyterian Church and Cumberland Presbyterian Church in America, consisting of ordained ministers and elders elected to represent sessions within a defined area.

Presbytery Board of Missions – Presbyterial board with responsibilities related to churches, pastor/church relationships, new church development projects, evangelism, and global missions. The regional Cumberland Presbyterian Women's Ministry is accountable to this board.

Presbytery Manual of Operations – Resource which brings together in one resource most of the guidelines and regulations that direct the life and work of the presbytery. It can be found online by clicking on the Publications link - www.cumberland.org/gao.

Presbytery Stated Clerk – Elected officer of the presbytery whose duties are to record all minutes in permanent form and to supply extracts from them when properly requested. The stated clerk shall perform the duties of the office of stated clerk during the meeting of the presbytery unless otherwise determined by the presbytery. The stated clerk will receive minutes from the Clergy Care Committee and include in the preliminary minutes as well as other administrative details that will help presbytery and the committee's work run smoothly.

Rules of Discipline – Section of the *Confession of Faith* setting forth procedures for dealing with misconduct or unusual situations within the church.

CHAPTER ONE:
PREACHING, CEUs, MENTORING, COMPENSATION

Preaching - The committee is responsible for monitoring the freedom of the pulpits in the presbytery. Ministers should be responsible in their preaching, but neither the session nor members of the congregation should be allowed to interfere with the ministers' freedom to preach the gospel.

- Offer seminars and workshops on preaching.
- Provide stipends for ministers to attend preaching conferences.
- Create an online group for weekly sermon preparation and conversation.
- Host a monthly breakfast or lunch for the purpose of sermon preparation and worship planning.
- The Discipleship Ministry Team offers worship resources written by and suggested by Cumberland Presbyterians for special Sundays in the CPC and in the church year. Visit the website for more— https://cpcmc.org/discipleship/worship-resources/

Continuing Education - The committee shall encourage the ministers of the presbytery to participate in programs of continuing education and shall work with the Ministry Council's PDMT and Memphis Theological Seminary in making such programs available.

- Contact the PDMT for information on organizing a continuing education event on the topic of Ministerial Ethics. A minister's participation in such training shows "due diligence" should an issue arise in their ministry. It also indicates the same responsibility on the part of presbyteries to hold these training events on a regular basis and require the ministers under their care to attend.

- The Discipleship Ministry Team offers continuing education opportunities for churches and presbyteries. Visit the website for more information – www.cpcmc.org/discipleshipblueprints/
- A suggested minimum standard is six CEUs every three years (typically 10 clock hours equals one unit). The committee will want to urge all the ministers in the presbytery to meet those standards. Maintain a record of ministers' continuing education by providing a form for annual report. (See Appendix "A") Committees may also utilize the continuing education form available on the PDMT website. PDMT will report to Clergy Care Committee chairpersons annually, or upon request by the committee any ministers in their presbytery who have recorded their CEUs in the online format.
- Personal Information Forms will now include a place for ministers to indicate when they have taken the Healthy Boundaries, a ministerial ethics training course provided by the PDMT.

Mentoring Newly Ordained Ministers – The first year of a newly ordained minister is an important time of growth and learning. It can also be a very challenging time. Assign a seasoned pastor with a new minister for the first 12-18 months of ministry. Responsibilities of the mentor may include:

- Monthly contact either face-to-face, email, or phone call. Check in with the minister to see how they are doing, and if there are any struggles, questions, or issues.
- Help facilitate an annual review with the session (using the Evaluation Tool available on the PDMT website). This evaluation tool reviews not only the minister but the work of the session as well.
- Take them out to lunch or invite them over for a meal, coffee, or dessert. If married include the spouse and/or children.
- Provide any support needed regarding record-keeping, tax filing, etc. This is not a time to inquire into pay, but an effort to help with keeping appropriate records, files, receipts, etc.
- Inquire as to their sabbath-keeping, days off per week, vacation time.

- Pray together on a regular basis.

Mentoring Ministers New to Presbytery – Often times ministers from other denominations are received into the presbytery. These people need support and mentoring as well. Assign a mentor to them for their first 12 months to help them assimilate into the life of the presbytery and denomination.

- Sit with them during meetings of presbytery. Answer any questions regarding the business and workings of presbytery.
- Follow up after presbytery, especially if there was business that needed action from the local church.
- Remind them of presbytery activities like CP Women's Ministry, Men's Fellowship, youth camps and retreats, synod.
- Encourage them to facilitate an annual review with the session (using the Evaluation Tool available on the PDMT website).
- Pray with them.

Compensation — Provide information for minister's salary structure. Be an advocate for just and fair compensation for ministers that helps to maintain the health of the pastoral relationship.

- Organize periodic seminars on financial health, planning for retirement, and ways to structure their salary package.
- Encourage ministers to participate in a group health insurance policy, in the denominational retirement program, and other resources that can benefit them financially.

Salary and Compensation

The information in this section is beneficial for a committee to know and share where and when appropriate with ministers, particularly those ministers who are newly ordained. These items are included in the contract sample. (See Appendix "B")

Base Salary — This item is determined by the value placed on ministerial leadership. Consideration is given to abilities, years and type of experience, special skills and education, the median income of the congregation, and duties of the job. It does not include comparison with the previous minister's salary or the previous salary of the incoming minister, except as it reflects the value each church places on leadership in ministry. Consideration of merit or annual cost of living increase, and other changing factors are necessary to each year's salary negotiations.

Housing Compensation — Housing compensation is part of the minister's compensation, whether by providing an allowance for housing expenses (mortgage, utilities, etc.) or a church-owned house. The housing allowance is determined by the actual cost of housing in the community where the church is located, or in a community wherein the members of the ministry setting reside.

Housing allowance generally includes rent or mortgage payments, utilities, taxes, insurance, maintenance, and home furnishings. The annual housing allowance needs to be approved by the church session. Specific IRS rules govern housing allowances for ministers; those rules change often. An annual tax guidebook is available through the Board of Stewardship and Benefits (call 901.276.4572, ext. 206)

Work Week — It is helpful to think of a workweek in units; rather than individual hours (example, each unit = four-hour block; morning, afternoon, evening). A 10-unit week (40 hr/wk) is recommended as optimal. A workweek of 13 units may at times be a reality but should be considered extreme, and compensatory time needs to be granted to the minister to balance their time and facilitate self-care.

Health Insurance — A local church needs to provide healthcare insurance for their full-time minister. Ministers can participate in the denominational insurance program. Many presbyteries help with the premiums. This program includes a separate vision and dental plan. While some ministers may be able to get health insurance coverage through the Affordable Care Act for their family and self, it is an act of care and support to provide that for them through a group plan.

Retirement Contribution – A local church needs to contribute on a matching basis into the denomination's retirement fund on behalf of their minister. Whatever percentage a minister contributes, the church matches up to a maximum 5%. In addition, the minister can contribute up to 15 percent of their base salary.

Long-Term Disability – This is a non-contributory plan, so presbyteries will make the contributions on behalf of the minister. Contact your presbytery to inquire about enrollment.

Social Security Allowance — Historically clergy have been classified for social security purposes as "self-employed." Internal Revenue Service rulings are changing. Ministers need to review the *Annual CPC Clergy Tax Guide* provided by the Board of Stewardship and Benefits and their personal accountant regarding this item. Some churches reimburse its minister for the portion of Social Security that a church would pay for a non-ordained employee.

Vacation and Days Off — Depending upon tenure, 2-4 weeks annually is recommended. Two days off per week is strongly encouraged to assure a minister's continued health and wholeness. Additional time may be given for conferences, continuing education, etc.

Continuing Education and Sabbatical Leave — The time and expense incurred in maintaining and renewing the spiritual and vocational needs of the minister should be considered in the total salary package. Two weeks of continuing education a year is recommended. Sabbaticals are an important benefit to provide to long-term pastorates. After 5-7 years of service, a three-month sabbatical is typical. Ministers will often apply for a grant to help fund their sabbatical. They will need to retain their full salary and benefits during the sabbatical. There is often the expectation that a minister will commit to a set number of years of continuing service to the church following their sabbatical.

Sick Leave — Attention needs to be given to sick leave and emergency time off (family sickness, death, etc.) In developing a sick leave policy, a possible plan would allow one day for each full month of employment. Some presbyteries provide short-term disability benefits to their ministers. Check with your presbytery's Board of Finance for more details related to short- and long-term disability.

Maternity/Paternity Leave – A period of maternity/paternity leave is an important way for congregations to support a minister and family. Twelve (12) weeks of leave are recommended usually taken during the last weeks of pregnancy and first weeks after delivery. Details of the leave should be negotiated and clearly expressed in the call agreement and to the congregation to avoid misunderstandings.

Auto/Travel Reimbursement and Professional Expenses — The minister incurs these expenses on behalf of the congregation. It is not to be considered income to the minister because it is congregational ministry such as hospital visits, home visits, travel to meetings (which may include lodging and meals), resource books, stoles, robes, etc. Therefore, it is recommended that this be a line item in another part of the church budget and be treated as a reimbursable line item.

Annual Review — The session or personnel committee needs to review with the minister the salary and benefits prior to preparing the budget for the next year.

A Sample Contract is available on the PDMT website for a minister/session to use when establishing a salary and benefits plan. (See Appendix "B")

CHAPTER TWO:
HEALTH AND ONGOING CARE

Marriage and Family – The committee should publicize and promote seminars for ministers and their families dealing with marital problems, marriage enrichment, and coping with the unique challenges of the ministerial family.

- Refer a minister to the presbytery's CONCERN Employee Assistance Program (EAP) for counseling. Benefits include unlimited counseling for the minister, family members and anyone living in the household. If your presbytery does not participate in the EAP, contact the PDMT office for more information on how to enroll. Partner with a local or regional counseling group for a discounted fee if your presbytery continues to not participate in the EAP.
- Consider providing funds to help with counseling costs.
- Organize a presbytery seminar for ministers and their families on the joys and challenges of the ministry. Invite "seasoned" spouses to tell their stories, include PKs (Preacher's Kids) on the program, a speaker on the "fishbowl" ministry, among other topics.

Mental Healthcare - The committee shall encourage ministers and/or spouses who are having trouble coping to seek professional help. The committee should provide information concerning the availability of such help and where possible, provide financial aid for counseling services.

- If your presbytery participates in the Employee Assistance Program provide information to the minister on how to access the benefits. As a participating presbytery, a minister and their family (and anyone living in the home) have free, unlimited access to counseling.

- For more information regarding the EAP and how to enroll if your presbytery does not participate, contact the office of the PDMT.
- Encourage all ministers in the presbytery to observe a regular sabbath day.
- Support the spiritual well-being of ministers to help prevent burn-out, cynicism or even anger at the disappointments of ministry. Organize a day of sabbath rest for the ministers in your presbytery. Share with them opportunities for spiritual retreats and conferences as you discover them.

Ongoing Care of Ministers – As a committee, it is helpful to hold a mirror up before the ministers under your care to call attention to the many areas of their lives that need attention – spiritual, emotional, relational, financial, physical, etc. There are small ways in which you can support a minister in each of these areas throughout the year.

- Provide a lending library on topics of well-being; give away a couple of books at each meeting of presbytery on a different area; share online resources throughout the year.
- Create a common book list from ministers in the presbytery who would be willing to share their books with others, including probationers. The committee would keep this book list and provide it annually at presbytery meeting.
- PDMT will create a common reading list each year and post it on the website, in *The Cumberland Presbyterian,* and social media outlets.
- Provide information on how to apply for a sabbatical grant. A good resource can be found at the Lilly Endowment (www.lillyendowment.org).
- Host a one-hour seminar at your fall meeting of presbytery led by a tax account familiar with clergy/church taxes.
- Provide information on marriage enrichment opportunities in your area or talk with your EAP provider about a speaker for an event in your presbytery.
- Set up an emergency crisis fund for situations such as termination, temporary unemployment, or medical crisis. The PDMT has a Clergy Crisis Fund that the presbytery might want to consider if a minister is in dire financial need. Circumstances for which benefits can be approved include death in the

immediate family, out-of-pocket medical expenses, counseling, termination (one-time expenditure), or other considerations taken under advisement. A Clergy Care Committee or Committee on the Ministry, a stated clerk, a presbytery, or an individual minister can request funds on behalf of someone. No payment will exceed $1000 per year. More information can be found on the PDMT website.

- There may be occasions when a minister wishes to revoke their ordination. The committee should provide counsel to the minister. After counsel, if the minister still desires to revoke their ordination, the committee will make that report to the presbytery, which will then act upon the report ("Constitution," 6.53). This minister can now be received as a member of a particular church upon reaffirmation of faith (Constitution," 6.54).

CHAPTER THREE:
LEADERSHIP REFERRAL SERVICES (LRS)

This is a service of the PDMT and is available to churches who are searching for a new pastor and for ministers who may be searching for a call. It is an online, automated process whereby churches and pastors can connect with each other. It is a confidential process and ministers can remain anonymous until they are ready to let their identity be known to an inquiring church. PDMT has requested that all ministers complete an online profile, even if they are not in an active search process. The reason for this request is an effort to make room for the movement of the Holy Spirit through technology. A minister never knows when God's Spirit will move within them to consider a new/different call.

- **LRS webpage** — www.cpcmc.org/pdmt/lrs/
- **LRS online** — www.lrs.cpcmc.org
- **Personal Information Form** (PIF) — Pastors are encouraged to update their PIF every 5 years (or sooner if they are in an active search). Forms can be found on the LRS webpage. PDMT keeps PIFs on file but does not distribute them to churches unless directed by the minister.
- **Opportunity List** – A listing of churches that are in an active pastor search process and working through PDMT. This list is updated regularly and can be found at www.cpcmc.org/pdmt/opplist/.
- LRS sends out a **Monthly Email** to all the ministers in the CP church containing all the churches that are in an active pastor search process. This email contains the name of the search committee chairperson and a link to their email address.

CHAPTER FOUR:
CONFLICT MANAGEMENT

Conflict Management and Resolution – The committee is responsible for monitoring the ministries of the various pastors in the presbytery. When a problem arises, which cannot be resolved within the session, the committee should investigate the situation and seek to bring about reconciliation. If not possible, the committee should report the matter to the presbytery, making such recommendations as it deems advisable. It is preferable for the session to seek the committee's help in such situations, but if such an invitation is not forthcoming, the committee should initiate the action. Because problems involving the pastor also involve the congregation, it is important that the committee work closely with Board of Missions.

- Host a conflict resolution workshop for the ministers in the presbytery or join with the presbyterial Board of Christian Education/Discipleship to co-host such an event.
- If your presbytery participates in the CONCERN EAP, encourage ministers to take advantage of the counseling services provided.
- Be pro-active providing care for the ministers of the presbytery with a regular, periodic "check-in." Divide the ministers among your committee members and touch base with them by phone or in person every six months. It is easier to defuse a situation than to try and repair a broken relationship.
- Encourage all the ministers to facilitate with their session an annual review using the Evaluation tool on the PDMT website. Encourage them to do this on an annual basis, in an effort to deal with issues before they develop into a major conflict. Keep in mind, when a pastor/congregation is in the midst of a conflict is NOT the time to do an evaluation, especially if they've never done one before.

Discipline – The committee shall investigate reports coming to it concerning ministers who flagrantly disregard the provisions of the "Constitution" and/or preach and teach doctrines contrary to the creedal statement of the church. Report to the presbytery situations which may call for the disciplining of a minister. The procedures for handling such cases are stated in the "Rules of Discipline," section 3.400 – Discipline of Ministers.

CHAPTER FIVE:
CHURCHES WITHOUT MINISTERS

Elders as Communion Celebrants – In a church without an installed Cumberland Presbyterian minister the session will "designate two elders, either of whom, when authorized by the presbytery, may administer the sacrament of the Lord's Supper to the congregation provided they have been instructed in the meaning of the sacrament and how it should be administered. The elders shall serve under the authority of an ordained Cumberland Presbyterian minister selected by the presbytery, and each grant of authority shall be for one year (Constitution, 4.6).

The Committee on Clergy Care (or Committee on Ministry/Preparation) will facilitate the necessary training to those elders using *the Workbook for Training Elders as Communion Celebrants* available through the CP Resource Center (8207 Traditional Place, Cordova, TN 38016) or by visiting the online bookstore – www.cpcmc.org/store-2/.

Certified Lay Leaders – This often under-utilized and misunderstood role lies within the responsibilities of either the Committee on Ministry Preparation or the Committee on Clergy Care. A designated elder may provide leadership and support to a congregation other than their own. The elder, along with the session, may provide pastoral oversight of the congregation in the following ways:
- Give particular attention to persons who have not confessed Jesus Christ as Lord and Savior;
- Instruct persons in the faith;
- Visit people in their homes and in hospitals, praying with and for them;

- Encourage people by word and example to share in the worship, study, witness, and service of the church;
- Supervise the work of the deacons;
- Give oversight to the educational program of the church;
- Encourage stewardship, provide for the collection of monies for godly purposes, and supervise the finances of the church;
- Assemble the congregation and provide for worship. (*Minutes of the General Assembly of the Cumberland Presbyterian Church,* 1988, page 179).

There is a handbook to help with training Certified Lay Leaders, *Elders Serving as Lay Leaders in Small Congregations* available through the CP Resource Center.

CHAPTER SIX:
PASTOR APPRECIATION IDEAS

The second Sunday in October is typically set aside for this observance. It is a bit awkward for a minister to suggest his or her own appreciation, so this is where a committee can really take the lead. Send out a notification to all the churches in your presbytery via the mail/email list that your clerk keeps. Most presbyteries are happy to forward any communication from presbyterial boards. Remind churches of this day – then offer ideas on how to show appreciation and thanks. Here are a few ideas to spark the committee's creativity:

- Dinner and movie (and free childcare if they have children). If the minister is single, then dinner and movie for two!
- Organize a fellowship lunch and collect a love offering.
- Children of the church can make cards.
- Tickets to a sporting event or the theater.
- A weekend getaway.
- Give them a Sunday off and get elders to take care of all the worship details including the sermon, which will give them the opportunity to participate as a worshiper, which is a rare experience.
- Arrange for their car to be detailed.
- Give them a bunch of gift cards to restaurants, bookstores, movie theaters, etc.

The Committee on Clergy Care serves as a role model to the churches by showing appreciation of ministers under your care. Hold a *Get-Away-Weekend* drawing twice a year during the presbytery meeting. Send a letter inviting session clerks to share the communication with the session nominating the pastor for an all-expense paid weekend (2 nights lodging, meals, and transportation anywhere within the bounds of your presbytery).

The letter should explain that the presbytery will conduct a special drawing of names at next the meeting. The letter stipulates that the nomination from the session must include a paragraph detailing what they appreciate most about their pastor. The session also agrees to grant on behalf of the congregation an ADDITIONAL Sunday off for the pastor, not to be considered either as vacation or study leave, if selected in the drawing for this *Get-Away-Weekend*.

The Committee on Clergy Care asks the sessions to turn in their nominations to them at least a week before the presbytery meeting for the drawing. During the presbytery meeting, the drawing is preceded by a conversation about the importance of congregations caring for their clergy persons.

Following the presbytery meeting, the Committee on Clergy Care will send a letter to every pastor who was nominated for the drawing, along with the words of appreciation the session had written about her or him, expressing the presbytery's joy and gratitude for the good work she or he is obviously doing in the church.

The funds for the *Get-Away-Weekend* come from the Committee on Clergy Care's budget. The Committee might start with this expression of appreciation just once a year. This money is well spent and helps to emphasize both the presbytery's recognition of the work that pastors are doing and the Committee on Clergy Care's efforts as well.

For those pastors who are not serving a particular congregation, care will need to be given to find ways to support them in their ministry context.

Recognition of Milestones is a meaningful way to support the ministers. Send cards, emails, or make phone calls to ministers upon significant occasions such as ordination anniversaries, birthdays, wedding anniversaries, retirements, educational degrees/graduations, marriage, and births to name a few.

- One way to gather this important information is to ask ministers to complete an annual profile every year to record those dates. You can also gather CEUs at this time as well as special prayer requests.

PDMT will prepare a commendation upon the retirement of the minister when notified. With a donation to the Legacy of Ministry Endowment, PDMT will provide a certificate at the time of retirement. More information is provided under the Legacy of Ministry section in this manual.

CHAPTER SEVEN:
LEGACY OF MINISTRY RECOGNITIONS

This legacy is established in recognition of the faithful and passionate ministries of Samuel McAdoo, Finis Ewing, Samuel King, and Louisa Woosley. These ministers created a legacy of ministry that countless Cumberland Presbyterian ministers have continued down through the years. By participating in this legacy, honorees and donors will become coworkers with the churches' foremothers and forefathers who carried the good news of Jesus Christ to the frontier.

- **Legacy of Ordination** – A gift of $100 at a person's **ordination** will include them in this legacy. They will receive a certificate suitable for framing and a cross pendant with cord. A minister who is already ordained can chose to participate in this legacy with a $100 donation in recognition of their own ordination and will receive the pastoral cross.
- **Legacy of Retirement** – A gift of $100 at the time of a minister's **retirement** by a presbytery, church or person will give recognition to the minister and their services to the church. With the recognition comes a certificate suitable for framing and a commendation. Please complete the "Retirement Commendation Form" found on the PDMT website when requesting this recognition.
- **Legacy of Ordination Anniversary** is an opportunity for ministers and those who support them in their ministry to celebrate this annual milestone. Donations can be made depending upon the number of years ordained (ex. to celebrate the 37th year of an ordination a contribution is made in the amount of $37 to the Legacy Endowment). The honoree will be

notified of any donations made in their honor. All donors will receive a letter of thanks for continuing the Cumberland Presbyterian Legacy of Ministry.

- Gifts to this legacy at the **death** of a minister will continue the legacy for years to come. The family will receive notification of donations on behalf of their loved one.
- **Appreciation donations** will be welcomed any time of year, but especially during the month of October when Pastor Appreciation is often observed.
- For more information regarding the Legacy of Ministry visit the PDMT website or call the office at 901.276.4572, x203. (See Appendix "C").

CHAPTER EIGHT:
IMPORTANT MISCELLANEOUS ITEMS

Annual Reports – Require annual reports from ministers whose ministry is not under the jurisdiction of the presbytery. Presbytery has responsibility to require that all ministers engage in the work of the church unless honorably retired or excused by the presbytery.

- Report to the presbytery annually the type of ministry in which each minister on the presbytery roll is engaged. Presbytery has responsibility to review and possibly approve the work of ministers who are not engaged in generally recognized forms of ministry.
- Receive and review annual reports from the sessions on the pastors' compensation, and present to presbytery requests for changes in terms of the pastors' calls.
- Prepare annual necrology report for the memorial service at presbytery. Consider making a donation to the Ministry of Legacy in memory of those ministers who have died.

APPENDIX A:
CONTINUING EDUCATION REPORT FORM

Name _____

Street Address _____

City _____

State _____ Zip _____

Email _____

Mobile Phone _____

Landline _____

Presbytery _____

Current Ministry Setting _____

(1 clock hour = 0.1 Continuing Education (CEU)

Event:	
Location:	
Event Date:	
Total # of Clock Hours:	
Total # of CEUs:	

Event:	
Location:	
Event Date:	
Total # of Clock Hours:	
Total # of CEUs:	

Event:
Location:
Event Date:
Total # of Clock Hours:
Total # of CEUs:

Event:
Location:
Event Date:
Total # of Clock Hours:
Total # of CEUs:

Event:
Location:
Event Date:
Total # of Clock Hours:
Total # of CEUs:

Event:
Location:
Event Date:
Total # of Clock Hours:
Total # of CEUs:

APPENDIX B:
PROPOSED CONTRACT

This is a contract between the session of _____ Church and
the Reverend _____.

The _____ Church is sufficiently satisfied with the
qualifications of the Reverend _____ to serve as
_____ to enter into this contractual agreement.
_____ Church further believes that the Reverend
_____ by experience, training, disposition, and
commitment is especially suited to serve in this leadership position.

It is the intention of _____ Church to extend to the
Reverend _____ a call to assume the position of
_____ beginning on _____, and continuing for
an indefinite period of time; and it is the intention of the Reverend
_____ to accept this call and for both parties to accept the
following stipulations and agreements, namely:

(1) that the _____ Church does hereby promise the
     Reverend _____ in the discharge of duties that relate
     to this position, all proper support and encouragement;

(2) that the _____ Church does hereby obligate itself to
     pay the Reverend _____, in consideration of the services

to be rendered, the sum of _____ per month for base salary;

(3) that the _____ Church obligates itself to provide a manse, with utilities, for the Reverend _____ (or obligates itself to provide the sum of _____ per month for a housing allowance);

(4) that the _____ Church agrees to contribute on a matching basis up to 5 percent of the base salary into the denomination's retirement fund account of the Reverend _____;

(5) that the _____ Church agrees to pay the _____ (indicate family or individual coverage) medical insurance premium of the denomination's approved medical insurance program for the Reverend _____;

(6) that the _____ Church agrees to reimburse the Reverend _____ the sum of _____ per month for automobile expense;

(7) that the _____ Church agrees to provide the expense of moving the household effects of the Reverend _____;

(8) that the Reverend _____ be allowed a maximum of _____ weeks' time annually for vacation, and that the _____ Church be responsible for the cost of pulpit supply during the _____ Sundays involved; (many churches give a maximum of four weeks for pastors who have been serving in the denomination for ten years or more. Some churches also give an additional week or more for continuing education purposes.)

(9) that the Reverend _____ be allowed a maximum of _____ weeks annually for conferences, preaching missions, revivals, and/or other events (with the exception of judicatory responsibilities) that involve being away from the local community and/or local responsibilities, with the cost of pulpit supply being paid from a line item for this purpose in the church budget;

that the Reverend _____ be allowed _____ day(s) weekly (excluding Sunday) for time off, with day(s) being chosen by the Reverend _____ and being the same day(s) each week, so that the congregation may know the work schedule and call on his or /her services during time off only for crisis situations;

(10) that the Reverend _____ be allowed sick leave and emergency time off (family sickness, death, parental, etc.) within reasonable limits, and this be reviewed as necessary by the church session. (*Guidelines for suggested leave time are available from the Missions Ministry Team*);

(11) that the _____ Church agrees to review the salary and benefits promised the Reverend _____ at least annually prior to preparing the budgets for the next year;

(12) that this contract be for an indefinite period of time, with either party having the privilege and power to terminate it upon the giving of a minimum thirty (30) day notice of intention and desire to do so; and

(13) that this contract be entered into with the earnest hope and prayer

of all concerned that God will bless the relationship to which the

_____ Church and the Reverend _____

commit themselves by their signatures to this contract, arrived at

this _____ day of _____, A.D. _____.

_____   _____

(name) Clerk of Session   (name)

for _____ Cumberland Presbyterian Church

Session, Date signed: _____

by official action on the _____ day of _____, 20_____.

APPENDIX C:
CUMBERLAND PRESBYTERIAN MINISTRY OF LEGACY

This Legacy is established in recognition of the faithful and passionate ministries of Samuel McAdoo, Finis Ewing , Samuel King, and Louisa Woosley. These ministers created a legacy of ministry that countless Cumberland Presbyterian ministers have continued. By participating in this legacy ministers become co-laborers in building up the kingdom of God both now and in the future.

The Legacy of Ordination recognition is bestowed upon a newly ordained person by a presbytery or person with a gift of $100 to the Legacy. With the recognition, a minister will receive a certificate suitable for framing and pastoral cross pendant with cord. A minister who is already ordained can chose to participate in this Legacy with a $100 donation in recognition of their own ordination and will receive the pastoral cross.

The Legacy of Retirement recognition is bestowed upon a minister a retirement with a gift of $100 to the Legacy by a presbytery, church, or person. With the recognition comes a certificate suitable for framing and a commendation. Please complete the "Retirement Commendation Form" found on the PDMT website when requesting this recognition.

The Legacy of Ordination Anniversary is an opportunity for ministers and those who support them in their ministry to celebrate this annual milestone. Donations are made depending upon the years ordained. The minister will be notified of any donations made in their honer . All donors will receive a letter of thanks for continuing the Cumberland Presbyterian Legacy of Ministry.

Name of Person Being Recognized _____

Address _____ City _____ State ____ Zip ____

Current Presbytery _____ Current Date _____

Ordination Date _____ Ordaining Presbytery _____

Name and Dates of Churches Served or Other Ministry Settings _____

_____

_____

Offices Held _____

_____

_____

Application sent in by: _____ Date to be presented: _____

Where presentation will take place: _____

Please mail certificates/cross to: _____

Address _____ City _____ State ____ Zip _____

Ordination Legacy ($100) $ _____

Retirement Legacy ($100) $ _____

Ordination Anniversary Legacy (Amount Varies) $ _____

Pastoral Appreciation Donation (Amount Varies) $ _____

Gift upon Death (Amount Varies) $ _____

TOTAL AMOUNT ENCLOSED $ _____

Complete the form above and return with check payable to "Pastoral Development Ministry Team," 8207 Traditional Place, Cordova, TN 38016.

www.ingramcontent.com/pod-product-compliance
Lightning Source LLC
Chambersburg PA
CBHW031531040426
42445CB00009B/477